ABCs  OF BUGS

St. Clair Shores, Michigan

By Elizabeth Gauthier

I0:73455

For information about permissions
please write Gauthier Publications at:

Gauthier Publications
P.O. Box 806241
Saint Clair Shores, MI 48080
Attention: Permissions Department

Frog Legs Ink is an imprint of Gauthier Publications
www.FrogLegsInk.com

Proudly printed and bound in the USA

ISBN: 978-1-942314-87-5

Library of Congress information on file

Blue Words

You will see some words in this book are blue. That means they are special. You might not recognize them or know what they mean, but that's ok, there is a section in back that explains them. Then you can tell your friends all about a chrysalis or how some insects eat wood....it's true they do...go read about it in the back of the book!

Aa

Ant
I can lift 1000 times my weight!

Bb

Blue Orchid Bee
I help flowers and crops grow!

Cc

Caterpillar

When I'm ready, I make my own little
house called a Chrysalis and stay there
until I'm ready to fly away as a butterfly!

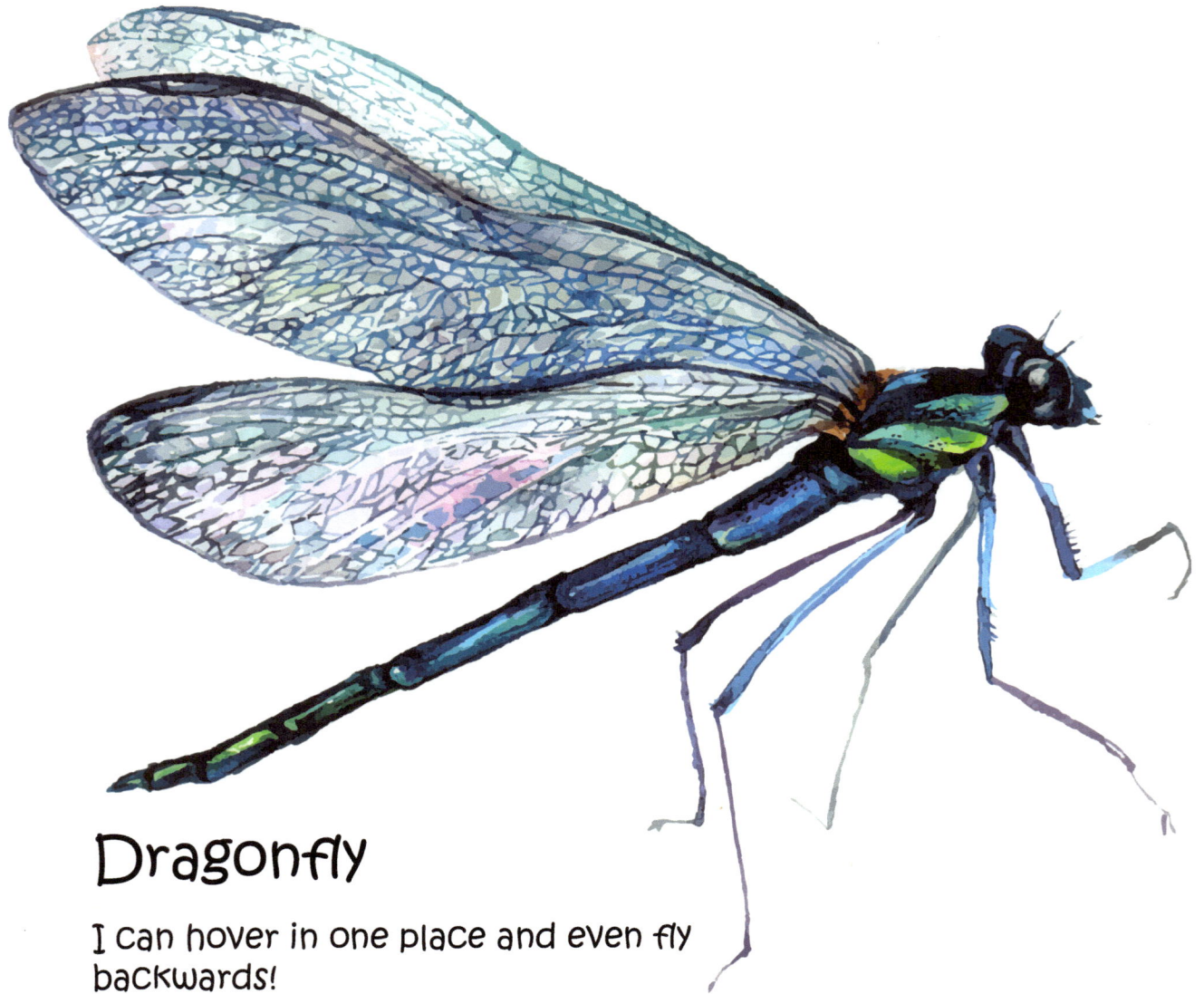

Dd

Dragonfly

I can hover in one place and even fly backwards!

Ee

Elephant Hawk Moth
When I'm a caterpillar, I am gray!

Ff

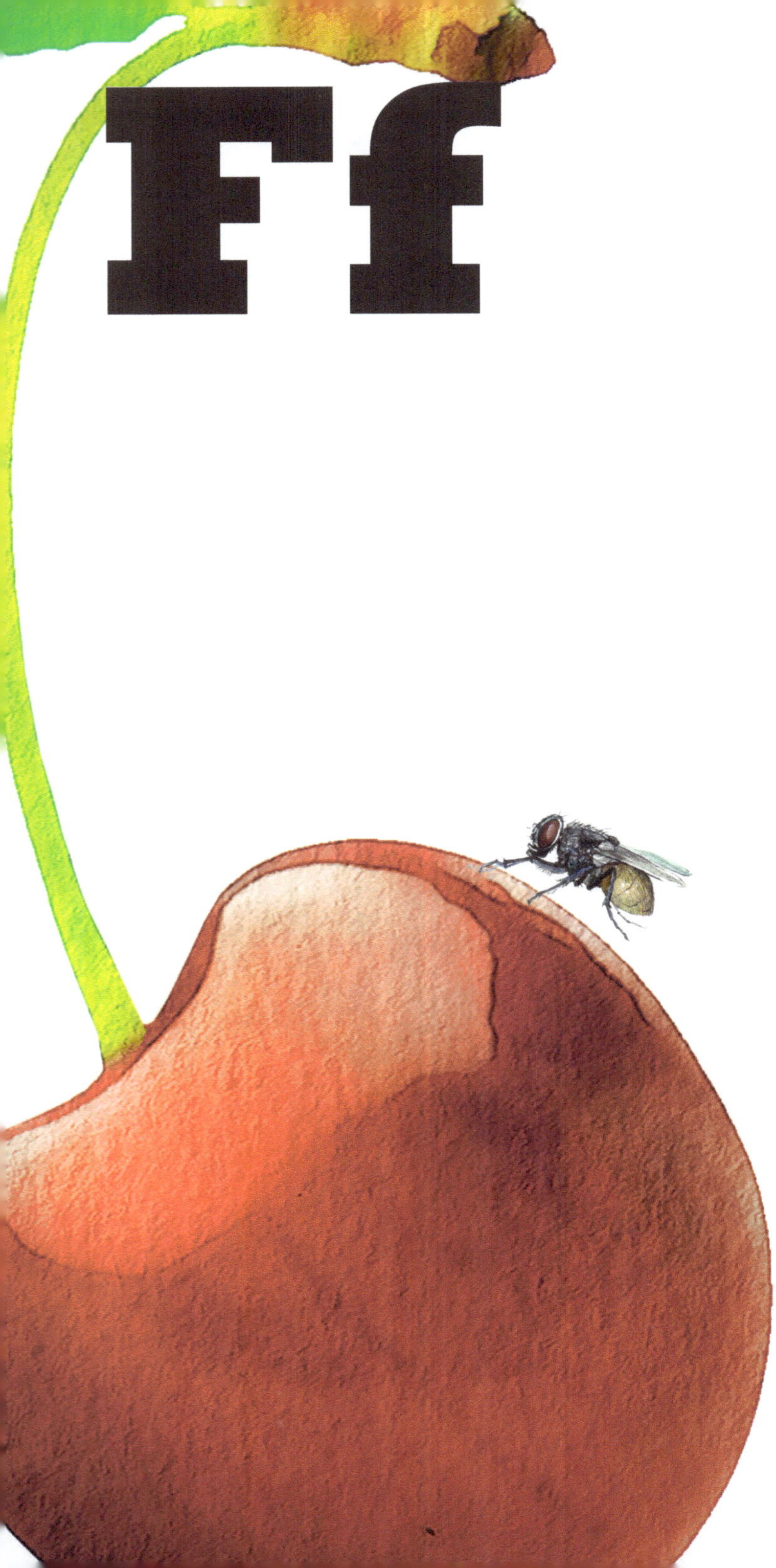

Fruit Fly

I love fruit, especially old fruit!

G g

Giant Stag Beetle

I am over 2 inches long! I like to drink tree sap!

Hh

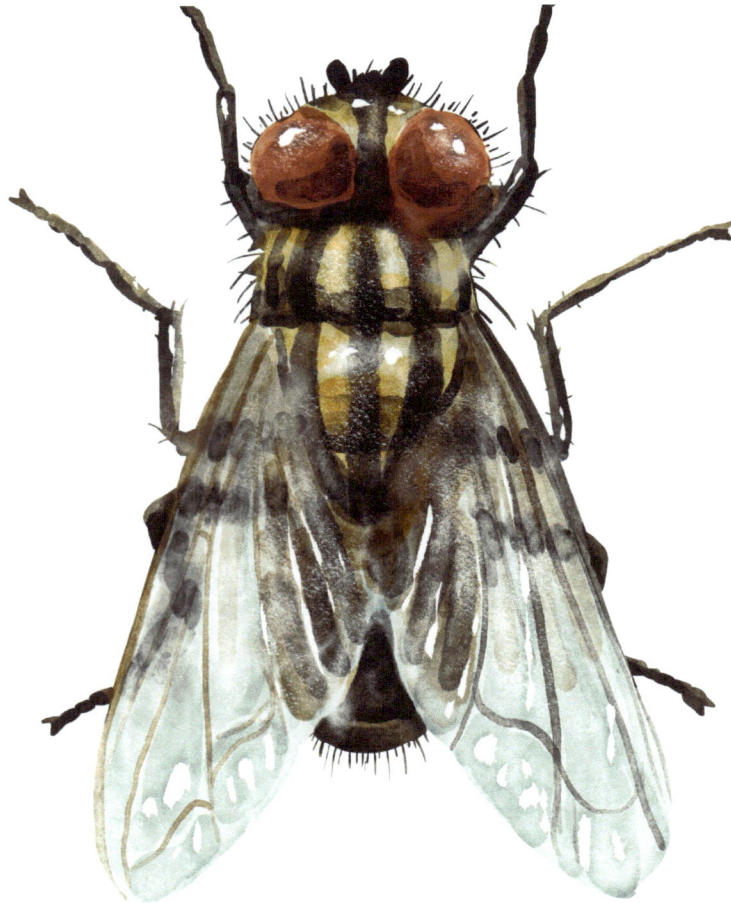

House Fly

My eyes are made of thousands of tiny lenses!

Ii

Inchworm

I only have feet on the
front and back of my body.
I have a unique way I move!

Jj

June Bug

When I need to protect myself
I make a hissing sound!

Kk

Katydid

I blend in with tree leaves for protection. Sometimes I'm called a leaf bug!

Ll

Lady Bug

I hide my wings!

Mm

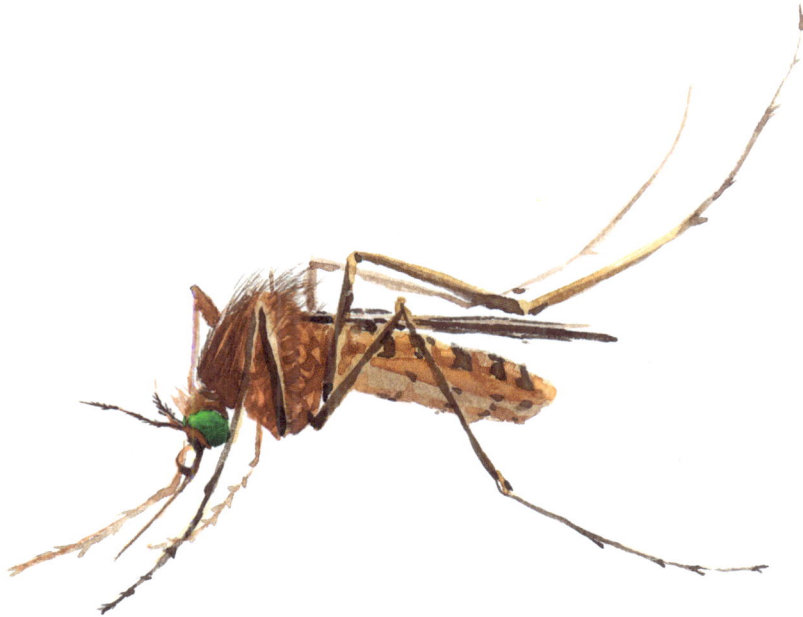

Mosquito
I drink blood!

Nn

Nightcrawler

I live in the dirt and help things grow!

Oo

Owl Butterfly

When I close my wings
I look like an owl!

Pp

Praying Mantis

Unlike other insects, I can turn my
head from side to side!

Qq

Queen Bee

I lay lots of eggs!

Rr

Rhinoceros Beetle

I have a big horn on my head!

Ss

Scarab

I was very popular
in ancient Egypt!

Tt

Tiger Beetle
I'm a very fast runner!

Uu

Ulysses Butterfly
I live in the rain forest!

Vv

Venus Fly Trap

I'm not a bug. I'm a plant...
who loves to eat bugs!

Ww

Winged Ant

I grow wings during part of my life!

Xx

Xylophagous

That big word means I'm
an insect that eats wood.
I am a termite!

Yy

Yellow Jacket

I help plants by eating other insects that can hurt them!

Zz

Zebra butterfly

I have beautiful stripes on my wings!

Blue Words

Blue Orchid Bee: A pretty blue color, these bees are better and more efficient pollinators of local crops

Chrysalis: Also called a pupa, a Chrysalis often can be seen hanging from a branch. Inside the caterpillar is changing into a butterfly and, when ready, will fly away.

Venus Fly Trap: This is a carnivorous plant (this means they eat bugs). Once the plant senses a bug, their trap closes quickly so they can digest it. If a seed or leaf get in the trap and it closes, the Venus Fly Trap will spit it out!

Xylophagous: This term means that the bugs eat wood. Many have pinchers they use to bite and dig tunnels into wood.

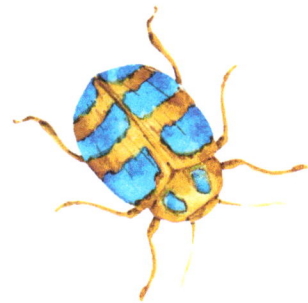

ABCs OF HALLOWEEN
By Elizabeth Gauthier

ABCs OF THE SEA
By Elizabeth Gauthier

ABCs OF BABY ANIMALS
By Elizabeth Gauthier

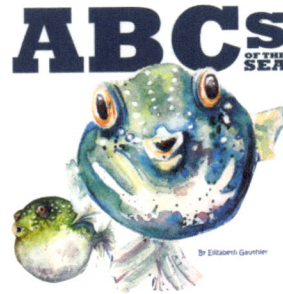

Look for
additional activities
& lesson plans!

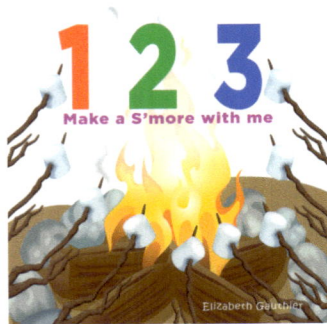

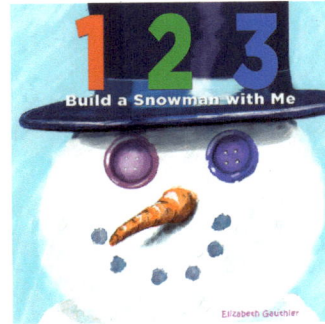

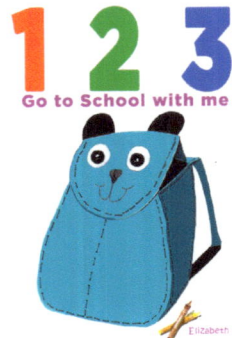

1 2 3 Make a S'more with me
Elizabeth Gauthier

1 2 3 Build a Snowman with Me
Elizabeth Gauthier

1 2 3 Visit the circus with me
Elizabeth Gauthier

1 2 3 Go to School with me
Elizabeth Gauthier

1 2 3 Carve a pumpkin with me
Elizabeth Gauthier

1 2 3 Make a Banana Split with me
By Elizabeth Gauthier

www.ingramcontent.com/pod-product-compliance
Lightning Source LLC
Chambersburg PA
CBHW042117040426
42449CB00002B/75